Contents

1 Rich people at home

Source A

Queen Victoria reigned between 1837 and 1901. At this time Britain was the richest country in the world. British industries sold goods all over the world. British ships carried most of the goods the countries of the world wanted to trade with each other. This meant that there were some very rich people living in Britain. Some men made their money in trade and industry. Others **inherited** wealth because their families owned land and property.

In 1850 a man who earned £1,000 a year lived a very comfortable life with his wife and family. He could pay for a large house and servants. Many men earned far more than £1,000. They had houses in the country and in London. They had many servants to look after them and their houses and **estates**.

This picture is a photograph of the drawing room of a house. The house was at Bushey, in Hertfordshire. It was lived in by W. S. Gilbert. He wrote plays and songs. There is a lot of furniture in the room. There are easy chairs and a sofa, a piano, tables and lamps, a vase of flowers and a potted plant, a decorated cabinet and lots of paintings, photographs and ornaments. Servants kept this room, and all the other rooms in the house, clean and tidy.

Life in
Victorian Britain

The Victorians
at Home

Heinemann

First published in Great Britain by Heinemann Library
an imprint of Heinemann Publishers (Oxford) Ltd
Halley Court, Jordan Hill, Oxford OX2 8EJ

MADRID ATHENS PARIS FLORENCE PRAGUE WARSAW PORTSMOUTH NH CHICAGO
SAO PAULO SINGAPORE TOKYO MELBOURNE AUCKLAND IBADAN GABORONE JOHANNESBURG

Designed by Ron Kamen, Green Door Design Ltd, Basingstoke, Hampshire
Colour Repro by Track QSP Ltd, London
Printed in Spain by Mateu Cromo Artes Graficas SA

99 98 97 96 95
10 9 8 7 6 5 4 3 2 1

ISBN 0 431 06669 8 [HB]

99 98 97 96 95
10 9 8 7 6 5 4 3 2 1

ISBN 0 431 06681 7 [PB]

British Library Cataloguing in Publication Data
Rees, Rosemary
  Victorians at Home. - (Life in Victorian Britain Series)
  I. Title II. Series
  941.081

Acknowledgements
The Publishers would like to thank the following for permission to reproduce photographs:
Barnaby's Picture Library: p. 6A
Bridgeman Art Library: p. 23B, p. 26A
Fine Art Photographic Library: p. 9C
Hulton Deutsch: p. 7B, p. 11C
The Illustrated London News Picture Library: p. 8A, p. 15C, p. 16A
The Mansell Collection: p. 14A
The Mary Evans Picture Library: p. 13B
National Monuments Record: p. 20A
The Tate Gallery: p. 29C

Cover photograph © Fine Art Photographic Library

Our thanks to Professor Eric Evans of the University of Lancaster for his comments in the preparation
of this book.

Every effort has been made to contact copyright holders of any material reproduced in this book. Any
omissions will be rectified in subsequent printings if notice is given to the Publisher.

Weights, measures and money

Victorians used a system of weights and measures that is not the same as the metric system
we use now. The system the Victorians used is called the 'Imperial' system.

Imperial measures

Length
1 inch [2.5 cm]
12 inches (1 foot) [30.0 cm]
3 feet (1 yard) [1.0 m]
1,760 yards [1.6 km]

Capacity
1 pint [0.56 litres]
8 pints (1 gallon) [4.50 litres]

Weight
1 ounce (oz) [28 grams]
16 oz (1 pound 'lb') [.45 kg]
14 lbs (1 stone) [6.3 kg]
28 lbs (1 quarter) [12.75 kg]
4 qtrs (1 hundredweight 'cwt')
  [50.00 kg]
20 cwts (1 ton) [1 tonne]

Area
1 acre [0.40 hectares]

Money
4 farthings = 1 penny (1*d*)
2 halfpennies = 1 penny (1*d*)
12 pennies = 1 shilling
        (1/- or 1*s*)
20 shillings = £1

Rich people spent a lot of time at home, or visiting other rich people. Sometimes the men had to go away from home to visit their lawyers or bankers, or to sit in the **House of Lords**. However, for most rich landowners their main job was to see that their estates were running well and making money.

Women and children

Rich women did not go out to work. They stayed at home. They made sure the servants did their work properly, and made their homes as comfortable as possible. Rich children stayed at home, too. They had lessons at home from a **governess** or a **tutor**. Only the boys went away to school when they were older. Rich people's homes were busy places, full of the comings and goings of the rich people themselves, and of their friends and relatives. They were full, too, of the servants who looked after them.

Source C

We rise early at half-past seven, have prayers at half-past eight, and breakfast a quarter of an hour later. After breakfast the children go to their schoolroom and Maria gives Kitty a music lesson. Aunt Catherine and I write or sew until eleven or twelve, when we go out driving (in a horse-drawn carriage). Uncle Richard goes shooting either by himself or with Mr Betton, and sometimes with Sir Charles Cuyler. We lunch when we return, and at six we dine. In the evening we form a very cheerful party by the drawing-room fire, reading, or sewing, or playing games with the children.

In 1851 an American girl, called Anna Maria Fay, visited her uncle on his estate in Shropshire. This is part of a letter Anna wrote home.

Source B

... outbuildings, gardens, greenhouses, hothouses; extensive fruit-walls, and the people labouring to furnish the table with fruit, vegetables and flowers; its coach-houses, harness-houses, stables and all the steeds, draught-horses, and saddle horses and ponies for the children; to see the waters for fish and the woods for game, and the elegant dairy for the supply of milk and cream, curds and butter. ... to enter the house and see the drawing-rooms; its steward's, housekeeper's and butler's rooms; its ample kitchens and larders, with their stores of provisions, fresh and dried; its stores of costly plate; its cellars of wine and strong beer; its stores of lines; its library of books ...

This is part of William Howitt's description of a rich man's house. He wrote it in his book, *Rural Life of England*, which was published in 1838.

Source D

Oh weary days – oh evenings that never seem to end. For how many years have I watched that drawing-room clock and thought it would never reach ten! And for twenty, thirty years more to do this.

Some women hated the sorts of lives they had to lead. A girl from a rich family, called Florence Nightingale (1820–1910), became a nurse. Before this, she was very, very bored at home. This is part of what she wrote about her life at home.

2 Middle-class people at home

Middle-class families lived comfortable lives. They had servants to look after them. Sometimes the servants lived in their homes too; sometimes they came in to work every day. Where a family could afford for servants to live in, they would live in a house with at least ten rooms. These were the kitchen, dining room, drawing room, library, three family bedrooms, two servants' rooms and a nursery. Even the poorest middle-class family had a servant of some kind. Often the servant was a girl of about twelve who helped to lay the fires, cook the meals and do all the washing.

A family like this would lived in a six-roomed **terraced house**, and would hope for something better when the man of the house earned more money.

Privacy

Victorian middle-class people thought of their homes as specially private places where families could be together. They put heavy curtains at their windows so that people walking in the street could not look in. They built high brick walls around their gardens so their neighbours could not see what was going on. Victorian middle-class homes were cosy, comfortable and private.

Source A

This photograph, called *The New Baby*, was taken in 1880. Many Victorians thought that middle-class, respectable family life was very important, and photographs like this were popular. Most Victorian women had a baby nearly every year. Having babies was a bit easier after about 1853, when women began to use **chloroform** to make childbirth less painful.

This photograph is called *The Cat and the Goldfish.* It was published around 1860. It shows a happy, comfortable middle-class Victorian family. They are laughing at their pet cat and goldfish. Photographs like this were supposed to make people think that most Victorians lived sensible, respectable lives, like this family.

Source C

The thought of the pain we had to endure from our clothes makes me even angrier now than it did then. The ladies never seemed at ease. Their dresses were always made too tight. Corsets were real instruments of torture; they stopped me from breathing and dug deep holes into my softer parts on every side.

When Gwen Raverat was an adult she remembered what it was like to wear Victorian clothes. She wrote about this in her book, *Period Piece*, which was published in 1954. In the 1880s middle-class Victorian women wore crinolines, which were dresses with skirts spread wide over light frames. Under her crinoline, a middle-class Victorian woman wore a vest, corsets stretching from her chest and over her stomach and hips, two or three petticoats and open-legged knickers.

3 Farmworkers' homes

Many farmworkers lived in cottages that went with their job. If they changed their job, they changed their cottage. A lot of these cottages were rotten. The walls were damp and the roofs let in water. The floors were made of earth. Large families lived in one or two rooms. They got water to wash in, to drink and to cook with from the village pond, or a pump or rain barrels. When someone wanted to go to the lavatory, they had to go down the garden to a **privy**. Four or five families often shared one privy.

Cottage life

Farmworkers owned very little furniture. Perhaps they had a couple of beds, some chairs and a table, a cupboard in which to put food and a chest for their clothes.

Some landowners provided well built cottages for their workers. Many farmworkers tried hard to keep their homes clean and their families well fed and clothed, even though they earned very little money.

Source B

Wretched houses piled here and there without any order – filth of every kind scattered about or heaped up against the walls – horses, cows and pigs lodged under the same roof with their owners, and entering by the same door – in many cases a pigsty beneath the only window of the dwellings – 300 people, 60 horses and 50 cows, besides hosts of pigs and poultry – such is the village of Wark.

In 1850 a correspondent of *The Times* newspaper described the village of Wark, in Northumberland, like this.

Source A

This picture of farmworkers' cottages was drawn in 1846. They were in the village of Whitchurch, Dorset.

This picture is called *Washing Day*. It was painted by Pierre Edouard Frere in 1878.

**Source
D**

In nearly all the cottages there was only one room downstairs. Many of these were poor and bare, with only a table and a few chairs and stools for furniture. In some cottages the rooms were bright and cosy, with dressers of crockery, cushioned chairs, pictures on the walls and brightly coloured hand-made rag rugs on the floor. There were pots of geraniums, fuschias and old-fashioned sweet smelling musk on the window sills.

Some of the cottages had two bedrooms, others only one, in which case it had to be divided by a screen or curtain to accommodate parents and children. Often the big boys of a family slept downstairs, or were put out to sleep in the second bedroom of an elderly couple. Except at holiday times, there were no big girls to provide for, as they were all out in service (working as servants).

Flora Thompson was born in 1876. When she was a child she lived in the village of Juniper Hill in Oxfordshire. In 1939 she wrote about her time there, in a book called *Lark Rise*. This is part of what she wrote about farmworkers' homes.

4 Working-class people at home in towns

Many towns and cities grew fast in the nineteenth century. One such city was Bradford in the West Riding of Yorkshire. In 1801, 13,264 people lived there. In 1831 the number had risen to 43,527. By 1851 103,786 men, women and children lived in the city. New factories, **mills** and all kinds of businesses were opening. Old ones were growing bigger. They needed more and more people to work in them. People moved into towns to work and they all needed somewhere to live.

New houses

At the beginning of Queen Victoria's reign, thousands and thousands of new houses were being built quickly and cheaply. Houses were built in long **terraces** or around square courtyards. Some builders built 'back-to-back' houses. These were cheap houses built in a block. Not only did houses share side walls, but they shared a back wall as well. Some houses were built well. Many, however, were built from cheap bricks, wood and tiles.

From about the 1860s many **town councils** made by-laws which said how new homes had to be built. The town council of Huddersfield in Yorkshire, for example, said that no back-to-back houses were to be built in the town.

Renting a house

The sort of house a working-class family lived in depended on how much **rent** they could afford to pay. Skilled workers could usually afford to live in a four-roomed house (two rooms upstairs and two rooms downstairs). Many unskilled workers could only afford a 'one-up-and-one-down' house.

By the end of the century, master builders employed teams of men to put up whole streets at a time. They bought windows, doors, fittings and fancy brick-work in bulk. These houses were built on empty land on the outskirts of towns and cities. In the 1880s these houses were rented by families who earned about £4 a week. Some of them could afford to employ one or two maids. The people who rented them had to travel in to work by **tram** or by train.

Source A

I visited the interior of nearly every cottage; I found all well, and many very respectably furnished: there were generally a mahogany table and chest of drawers. Most of the women were proud of their housewifery, and showed me the Sunday wardrobes of their husbands, the stock of neatly folded shirts. I found clocks and small collections of books in all their dwellings.

This is how William Cooke Taylor described the homes of some cotton workers in 1842. They worked in Ashworth's cotton mill at Turton, near Bolton, Lancashire, and lived near the mill.

We were poor but respectable. My father worked as a **drayman** for a public house about half a mile away from where we lived in Barnsbury Road, London. My mother took in sewing. I shared a bedroom with my two sisters, Alice and Rose. We all had our jobs to do, even when we were too young to go to school. I had to **black-lead** the **grates**. Alice had to clean all the vegetables for the day's meals and Rose, because she was the youngest, had to help mother with the washing. Upstairs we had poor Aunt Lizzie and her daughter Kate. Years later I found out that poor Aunt Lizzie had never married Kate's father. I never knew at the time. It was just something you didn't talk about. My parents gave them a home. No one said anything or thought it odd. It was just something families did to help. Otherwise they would have been out on the streets or in the **workhouse**.

Agnes Crane was born in London in 1884. In 1965 she wrote to her granddaughter to tell her what life was like when she was young. This is part of her letter.

This picture of the inside of a working-class home in London was drawn in 1872.

5 Slums

The poorest families could not afford to **rent** even the smallest house. They had to live, crammed in together, in single rooms wherever they could find them. There were large, old houses in the middle of most towns and cities. These were bought up by **landlords** and the large rooms were divided up into much smaller ones for really poor families to rent. Landlords even let out the cellars. Most of these landlords neither knew nor cared how their **tenants** lived. There was perhaps one water tap and one **privy** for as many as a hundred people. It did not take long for whole courtyards and streets to become **squalid** and filthy slums. These were places no respectable person would go.

This photograph of Market Court, Kensington, London, was taken at the end of the 1860s. There were thousands of courts like this in Victorian cities.

The government decided that something had to be done. In 1868 Parliament agreed to the first Artisans' Dwelling Act. This said that local councils could force a landlord to repair a house that was **insanitary**. If the landlord refused, the council could buy the house and pull it down.

Clearing slums

In 1875 Parliament agreed to the second Artisans' Dwelling Act. This gave councils the power to clear whole districts, not just single houses. Councils did not have to do these things: they could if they wanted to. Some did nothing because of the cost. Others, like Birmingham, began an enormous programme of slum clearance. Thousands of families were cleared out of city centres and left to find somewhere to live. It was only from about 1890 that councils had to find or build houses for these people.

We walk along a narrow, dirty passage into a square full of **refuse**. The windows above and below are broken. To the door comes a poor woman, white and thin and sickly-looking. She carries a girl; behind her, clutching at her scanty dress, are two or three other children. We ask to see the room. What a room! The walls are damp and crumbling, the ceiling is black and peeling off, the floor is rotten and broken away in places and the wind and rain sweep in through gaps that seem everywhere. The woman, her husband and her six children live, eat and sleep in this one room.

George Sims, who was a wealthy Londoner, went to see a London slum home in 1882. This is part of what he wrote about what he saw.

This is a picture of a slum home in Manchester. It was drawn in 1843.

Source B

6 Food: rich and middle-class people

Rich people ate a great deal of food. In most great houses, breakfast was served from about eight o'clock onwards. Lots of different dishes were put on a sideboard or side table. There would be eggs, bacon, grilled trout or turbot, grilled kidneys, cutlets, chops or steak and cold meats. There would be hot toast and different sorts of bread, butter, jam, tea and coffee.

Lunch and dinner

They ate luncheon around midday. This was a light meal of cooked meat or fish, or leftovers from the night before. Sometimes the husband ate luncheon at his **club**. His wife, then, would allow their children to come down from the nursery and eat with her. In the afternoon ladies went visiting and had afternoon tea with their friends. Dinner was served at around seven-thirty, and was more or less complicated, depending on whether or not the family had visitors. There were always servants to cook the food, serve the meals, clear everything away and wash it all up afterwards.

Source B

Soups
Consommé Desclignac   Bisque of oysters

Fish
Whitebait
Fillets of Salmon à la Belle-Ile

Entrees
Escalopes of Sweetbread à la Marne
Cutlets of pigeon à la Duc de Cambridge

Relevés
Saddle of Mutton
Poularde à la Crème
Roast Quails with Watercress

Entremets
Peas à la Française
Baba with Fruits   Vanilla Mousse
Croutes à la Française

This is the sort of dinner that rich people would have eaten in the 1890s. There would have been wine with every course, and coffee and **liqueurs** to finish with.

Source A

This picture of a Victorian dinner party was drawn in 1890.

This picture of a cook making the Christmas pudding in the kitchen of a middle-class home was drawn in 1848.

Housekeeping

In Victorian times many books were written about housekeeping. They were written for middle-class families who could afford one or two servants. In 1849, for example, a French chef called Alexis Soyer wrote a book called *The Modern Housewife*. In it he wrote hundreds of recipes and menus for middle-class housewives on different family budgets. By 1851 over 21,000 copies of the book had been sold. Most middle-class families, whatever their income, bought far more meat and fish than they did milk, fruit and vegetables.

Sunday
Pot au feu, fish, haunch of mutton, two vegetables, pastry and a fruit pudding, a dessert

Monday
Vermicelli soup, the bouilli of the pot au feu, remains of the mutton, two vegetables, fruit tart

Tuesday
Fish, shoulder of veal stuffed, roast pigeons, two vegetables, apple with rice and light pastry

Wednesday
Spring soup, roast fowl, remains of veal, minced, and poached eggs, two vegetables, rowley powley pudding

Thursday
Roast beef, remains of fowl, two vegetables, sweet omelet

Friday
Fish, shoulder of lamb, mirotan of beef, two vegetables, baked pudding

Saturday
Mutton broth, broiled neck mutton, liver and bacon, two vegetables, currant pudding

This weekly menu comes from *The Modern Housewife*. These are the sorts of meals a prosperous shopkeeper could probably have afforded to eat.

7 Food: working-class and poor people

In Victorian times many people tried to find out about the sorts of food eaten by working-class and poor people. Some of the people making the enquiries were doctors and some were journalists. They found out that there were differences between what working-class people in different parts of the country ate. At the beginning of Queen Victoria's reign, all working-class and poor people depended on bread and potatoes and ate very little meat at all. By about 1900, however, working people were eating far more meat and cheese than ever before.

Food in the countryside

In the countryside, labourers might have a bit of garden where they could grow vegetables. Many kept a pig which they fattened up during the year and then killed and ate. Some landowners provided their workers with fuel to burn; others gave the men beer to drink at lunchtime. However, food was often expensive to buy because there was usually only one village shop and the shopkeeper could charge what he liked.

Food in the town

Some town workers could not afford to cook more than two or three hot meals a week. For some, water to cook with had to be got from a tap in the street or yard. This tap was shared with many other people and was not always turned on. Many women, who were supposed to do the shopping and cooking, worked in factories and **mills.** On the other hand, there were far more shops in the towns than in the countryside, and people would have more food of different sorts to choose from. Food was often cheaper in the towns than in the country because shopkeepers competed with each other to sell their food and this kept prices down.

Source A

This picture of working-class people taking home their Christmas dinner was drawn in 1848. Many working-class people who lived in towns did not have proper kitchens. So they took their meat down to the local baker's shop and he cooked it for them in his bread ovens.

Buying food

At the beginning of Queen Victoria's reign many working-class and poor people had nowhere to store either uncooked or cooked food. This meant they bought their food on a day-to-day basis, and sometimes even from meal to meal. By the 1880s, however, things were changing. Shops were opening that sold lots of different sorts of food under one roof.

Liptons opened their first shop in Glasgow in 1871 and in Leeds in 1881; the first Sainsburys was opened in Croydon in 1882, and the Home and Colonial Stores opened in 1888. These stores aimed to sell good quality food cheaply. Soon there were branches in all the important towns and cities in Britain.

Source B

Breakfast at 7:	Parents – tea or coffee, with milk and sugar; bread and butter and cold meat Children – bread and milk
Dinner at noon:	Meat, bread, potatoes, vegetables; fruit or cheese
Tea at 4:	Tea, sugar, bread and butter
Supper at 8:	Remains of dinner

This is the food eaten by a **foundryman** and his family. He lived in Derbyshire with four children and his wife. He earned 27s 8d a week and spent 14s on food. Dr Edward Smith found this out. It is part of a survey he did for a report for the government in 1863.

Source C

After doing up his horses, he takes breakfast, which is made of flour with a little butter and water from the tea-kettle poured over it. He takes with him to the field a piece of bread and (if he has not a growing family and can afford it) cheese to eat at midday. He returns home in the afternoon to a few potatoes and possibly a little bacon, though only those who are better off can afford this. The supper very commonly consists of bread and water. Beer is given by the master in hay-time and harvest.

Between 1850 and 1851 James Caird made a survey of English agriculture. He was a journalist and worked for *The Times* newspaper. This is part of what he wrote about farm labourers in Dorset.

Source D

WILTSHIRE

Breakfast:	Water broth, bread and butter
Dinner:	Husband and children – bacon (sometimes), cabbage, bread and butter Wife – tea
Supper:	Potatoes and rice

LANCASHIRE

Breakfast:	Milk porridge, coffee, bread and butter
Dinner:	Meat and potatoes, or meat pie, rice pudding or a baked pudding; the husband takes ale, bread and cheese
Supper:	Tea, toasted cheese, and bacon instead of butter

These are examples of farm labourers' meals from different parts of England. They were collected by Dr Edward Smith.

8 Keeping clean and healthy

Everyone in Victorian Britain, whether they were rich or poor, needed water. Clean water meant that people could wash themselves and their clothes. Clean water meant that people could drink without getting ill.

Homes of the rich

Rich and well-off people had water running in pipes to their homes. All they had to do was turn on a tap in their own kitchens or bathrooms. They bought the water from water companies. However, the water did not run all the time. So most large houses had storage tanks in which they could store enough water for everyone in the house to use whenever they wanted.

Homes of the poor

Poor people did not have water piped to their houses until the end of the nineteenth century. Water companies put up **stand-pipes** in the streets. They sold water to poor people who had to queue, with buckets, saucepans and kettles, to take away the water they had bought. The stand-pipes did not always work. Then poor people had to get their water from streams, rivers and wells. Often this water was **polluted**. Poor people used as little water as possible because they could not afford it. Poor people in Victorian times found it hard to keep clean. Dirty, crowded living conditions meant that **disease** spread quickly.

Source A

DOULTON & CO., LAMBETH, LONDON S.E., PAISLEY & PARIS

THE LAMBETH
PATENT PEDESTAL
"COMBINATION" CLOSET

ADVANTAGES.

Front of Basin Lipped to form Urinal and Slop Sink when the seat is raised.

A water area equal to size of hole in seat, reducing the possibility of soiling basin.

Can be readily fixed, either square or across the corner of a room.

Self-contained, and all parts open to inspection.

Depth of water retained in basin, 1½ ins.

It may be flushed by simple seat-action arrangement, or by a pull handle as shewn.

THE LAMBETH PATENT PEDESTAL "COMBINATION" CLOSET are made both in STONEWARE, WHITE QUEENSWARE and STRONG GLAZED WARE. The former being especially adapted for places where they are liable to rough usage, as by reason of their great strength, they are less likely to be damaged.

THE WHITE QUEENSWARE are specially well finished and suitable for higher-class work.

These Closets are strongly recommended for HOSPITALS, ASYLUMS, PUBLIC INSTITUTIONS, FACTORIES, TENEMENTS, MODEL DWELLINGS. Also MANSIONS and PRIVATE HOUSES they are made both PLAIN & ORNAMENTAL and can be supplied either with Turned-down (S) Shoot-out (P) Trap.

THE WATER CLOSET—SLOP SINK—AND URINAL COMBINED.
This Closet has been designed by DOULTON & CO., and was awarded
THE GOLD MEDAL at the HEALTH EXHIBITION.

This advertisement for a lavatory was printed in the catalogue of Doulton and Co. in 1894. Only well-off people could afford one. When the lavatory was flushed, the contents went either into a **cesspit** in the house basement or into a **sewer**. Sewers and cesspits were emptied every so often by 'night-soil' men. Poor people had lavatories outside in courtyards and alleys. They did not flush. Their contents just tipped into cesspits which night-soil men sometimes emptied.

Source B

This drawing is called *Court for King Cholera*. It shows how easily cholera could spread in crowded, dirty slum courtyards. It was published in the magazine *Punch* in 1862.

Men, women and children usually had body **lice**. These lice spread **typhus fever**. There were **epidemics** of typhus in 1837 and 1839. Then in 1847, 10,000 people died from it in the north-east of England alone. Because people couldn't keep clean and lived crowded closely together, measles, 'flu and **scarlet fever** were often killers. People often had **diarrhoea**. However, the disease which terrified people was **cholera**. In Victorian times Britain was hit by three massive cholera epidemics: in 1848–9, 1853–4 and 1866. Cholera could kill a healthy person in 36 hours, and until the 1860s, no one knew how or why. In 1864 Louis Pasteur discovered that **germs** caused disease and that it was not disease that caused germs.

At the beginning of Queen Victoria's reign, very few people thought that the government ought to deal with health matters. By 1875 people had changed their minds. In 1875 a Public Health Act said that all **town councils** had to look after public health. Councils had to build sewers and run a safe water supply.

Source C

Sur,

May we beg and beseech your proleckshion and power. We are Sur, as it may be, livin in a wilderness so far as the rest of London knows anything of us, or as the rich and great people care about. We live in muck and filthe. We aint got no privez, no dust bins, no water suplies, no drain or suer in the whole place. The Suer Company in Greek Street, Soho Square, all great and powerful men, take no notice wat somedever of our complaints. The stenche of a Gully hole is disgustin. We al of us suffer and numbers are ill and if the Colera comes Lord help us.

This letter was published in *The Times* newspaper on 5 July 1849. It was signed by 54 people. The letter was badly spelled and not written by the kind of people likely to read *The Times*.
(Hint: read the letter out loud, quietly to yourself, if you can't understand it properly.)

9 Rich children at home

Rich children did not see very much of their parents. When they were babies they were looked after by nannies and nursemaids. Rich families had nurseries for their children. This was a room specially for them, where they ate, slept and played. They were visited by their parents. Usually the mother visited at tea time and sometimes ate nursery tea with her children. The father usually visited his children at bed-time, and sometimes read them a bed-time story. If both parents were at home, the nanny would bring them downstairs at the end of the afternoon to spend an hour with their parents. Children spent most of their time with the servants.

Many rich children found the **servants' hall** and the kitchen warm, comfortable and full of kindness and fun.

Playtime

Rich children had plenty of toys to play with. They had steam engines, soldiers, dolls, paints and drawing books. They had **clockwork** toys and toys that used sand or water to make the different parts move. Boys and girls were taught at home by a **governess**. Then the nursery was used as a schoolroom. When the boys were old enough they were sent away to school. The girls usually stayed at home and learned drawing, singing and French conversation.

Source A

This is a photograph of the nursery at Minley Manor, in Hampshire.

This is what happens in wealthy families: the children are confined to the third floor with their nurse; the mother asks for them when she wishes to see them and only then do the children come to pay her a short visit. When the nurse takes them down to her in the drawing room she looks to see that they are clean and have fresh clothes on. Once she has finished her inspection she kisses them and that is all until tomorrow.

Flora Tristan was a French lady. She visited London in 1839. She kept a journal which was published in 1842. This is from her journal.

This picture is called *The Children's Holiday*. It is a painting of Mrs Thomas Fairbairn and her children. It was painted in 1865 by William Holman Hunt.

My mother always seemed to me a fairy princess: a radiant being possessed of limitless riches and power. She shone for me like the Evening Star. I loved her dearly – but at a distance. My nurse was my **confidante**. Mrs Everest it was who looked after me and tended all my wants. It was to her I poured out my many troubles, both now and in my schooldays.

Winston Churchill was born in 1874. His father was Randolph Churchill, a rich politician and an aristocrat. In 1930 Winston wrote a book about his childhood, called *My Early Life*. This is part of what he said about his nurse and his mother.

10 Poor children at home

Poor families lived in small houses, often in just one room. This meant that brothers and sisters fought and cried, played and had fun, were sick and sometimes died, within sight and sound of each other, no matter what their ages. There were usually a lot of children, too. In Victorian times poor families had as many as eleven or twelve children.

Family life

Poor children in large families were often brought up by their elder sisters, and sometimes by their elder brothers. The mother couldn't possibly nurse a baby, watch a toddler who was just beginning to walk *and* keep an eye on children playing outside. Poor children didn't often have clothes made or bought for them. They wore clothes their older brothers and sisters had grown out of. When they, in turn, grew out of a dress or shirt, it was handed down to a younger brother or sister until it wore out and fell to pieces.

Working

Parents of poor children expected them to work for money as soon as they could. Sometimes they worked with their parents in the local cotton **mill**. Sometimes they worked away from their parents in the fields scaring birds or in the streets sweeping crossings or selling flowers.

Hunger and disease

Food was always a problem for poor children. Really poor families lived mainly on bread and potatoes, with sometimes a bit of bacon. In towns, poor children were sent to buy stale bread at the end of the day. Slightly better-off families managed to give their children meat and some vegetables on most days. Usually the father of a poor family had the best food. He earned the most money, and it was important that he was kept as strong and healthy as possible. Poor children were often hungry, and the food they did get wasn't always the best sort to help them grow and keep them healthy. This meant that they were often ill. In Victorian families it was usual for one or two children to die before they grew up. In poor families more children died because their parents could not afford to give them proper food, warm clothes and a comfortable home.

Source A

He was three days old before Emmy would look at him. Being the eldest, she had lots to do, and said there were enough to look after without another one. Father was very cross with her.

This comes from Anita Elizabeth Hughes' book, *My Autobiography*. She was born in 1892 near Lutterworth in Leicestershire. Her father was an estate gardener. Here she is describing how her elder sister Emmy behaved when their younger brother was born.

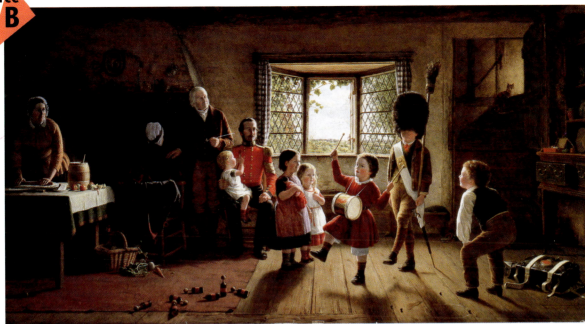

We always wore white pinafores and our dresses (made by Granny) always had a pocket at the side. If we showed our knees we were in trouble. We wore horrors called 'open drawers'. The two legs were made quite separately and only joined at the top with a top band which we fastened round the waist with a button and buttonhole. Thus it was very easy to smack little girls' bottoms. Mine was smacked so very often for giving a sulky look when asked to do something, for answering back or a childish argument (which happened often with seven children in the family). My mother would step in and punish both quarrelling children – to make sure she got the right one, she said.

Faith Dorothy Osgerby was born in Beverley, Yorkshire in 1890. Her father was a stonemason and she had six brothers and sisters. When she was seventy years old she wrote down all that she could remember of her childhood. This is part of what she remembered about being punished.

This picture of children playing at soldiers was painted by Frederick Hardy.

I remember being in bed with my brothers James and Robert. Suddenly I was taken out of bed and carried away to a cottage several miles distant by a friend of my mother's. I did not see my home again for six months. When I was brought home again, my playmates were gone. Black fever had almost emptied the house. During the time I was away my brothers, James and Robert, and my sisters, Mary-Ellen and Martha, had all died. As time went on, other children came to replace those who were lost. Robert (named after his dead brother) George, Thomas and Alfred.

William Webb was born in 1830 in East Kennet, Wiltshire. In about 1880 he wrote down what he could remember of his life. Here he remembers what happened when the black fever struck his family when he was a child.

11 Time off at home: rich and well-off people

Most rich and well-off people had one problem which they all shared. This was the problem of how to fill their time. The men and women did not have to go out to work in the same way that middle-class and working-class people did. Rich and well-off children had lessons at home until the boys went away to school. They had plenty of time to play at home. What did they do all day when they had time off from learning their lessons, making money, looking after their **estates** or visiting the poor and the sick?

Pastimes for men

Every large house had a study for the men. They would spend time there reading books, journals and the daily papers. They wrote letters to their banks and businesses. They wrote letters to the newspapers about things that interested them and matters they thought important, like the poor and fox-hunting. Some large houses had a billiard room with a full-size table, sets of cues and coloured balls. There the men would play billiards in the evening or when the weather was too bad to go outdoors.

Pastimes for women

Rich women learned a lot of skills when they were girls, and they used these to pass the time when they were adults. They sketched and painted; they played the piano and sang; they **embroidered** cushion covers and **fire screens**.

They went out for walks and carriage rides; they rode horses from the family stables. Whenever a lady left her home, a footman or other servant always had to go with her.

Most rich and well-off people lived in houses with large gardens. Adults used these gardens in their spare time. They played games like tennis and croquet; they took photographs of each other.

Rich people had a lot of visitors. Sometimes the visitors were married brothers and sisters, cousins and aunts. Sometimes the visitors were friends. Rich and well-off people had tea-parties in the afternoons and dinner parties in the evenings. They managed, one way or another, to fill their spare time at home.

Source A

I was born on 4 January 1885 in a lovely home called Ardleigh Court. The home was large and we had many servants. I remember to this day my love for horses grew as I became older. It hurt me so, as I was never allowed to go near the large stables unless someone came with me. We had a lovely pony to ride but someone always had to come with you.

Nora Mabel Nye remembers what it was like being a girl in the 1880s and 1890s.

This is a photograph of the garden of Cheyne House, Upper Cheyne Row, Chelsea in London. It was taken in about 1850. Look carefully and you can see a girl sitting on a rocking horse. She is sitting side-saddle. In 1850 Victorians thought it was not lady-like for women, and even girls in their own back gardens, to sit astride a horse – even a rocking horse. Look even more carefully and you will see two little chairs fastened on to the rockers of the horse. These were for the girl's younger brother and sister to sit in and to be rocked. Servants would have carried this rocking horse into the garden for the children to play with. Servants would have cleared everything up afterwards when the children went in for nursery tea.

May 18

This is a very busy day as we are going to have a party this evening, something larger than usual. We had four to dinner and about fifty or sixty in the evening. The company generally comes about ten or eleven o'clock and stays until one or two in the morning. Sweet-hearting matches are very often made up at these parties. It is quite disgusting to a modest eye to see the way the young ladies dress to attract the notice of the gentlemen. They are nearly naked to the waist, only just a little bit of dress hanging on the shoulder. Plenty of false hair and teeth and paint. If a person wishes to see the way of the world, they must be a gentleman's servant, then they might see it to perfection.

In 1837 William Taylor was a footman. In his diary he described a party that was held in the house where he worked. This is part of what he wrote.

12 Time off at home: working-class and poor people

Source A

In 1837 working-class and poor people did not often have spare time to relax and have fun at home. Men and women worked long hours in factories, **mills** and shops, down mines, on the railways and in the fields. When they got home they usually only had time to eat and sleep, ready for long hours of work the following day. By 1901, however, things had changed. In 1871 a Bank Holiday Act gave set days off work to everybody. Acts of Parliament had reduced the number of hours people were allowed to work. Working men, women and children had more spare time.

This picture was painted in 1856 by John Dawson Watson. He called it *Children at Play*.

Some working-class homes were comfortable and clean. Men and women enjoyed what little time they had at home. Many poor people lived in homes that were dirty, crowded and **squalid**. If they ever had any spare time, they certainly would not want to spend it at home.

This photograph of New Street, near Lambeth Dock, London, was taken in the 1860s. Poor children like these in the photograph did not have gardens to play in. They played in the street. It was not really dangerous. The traffic was horse-drawn and would have been slow. Mums, aunties and big sisters could sit on the doorsteps and watch the children so that they did not come to harm.

Source C

A miner never saw his home in daylight in winter except on Sunday. Sunday was not a working day in the Forest of Dean, but a day of rest and gladness. After tea father would get the **do-re-me board**, put it by the grandfather clock, and ask us to sing a hymn one by one, then we would all sing together with Father leading us. We always enjoyed that half-hour. In the summer we all went out on the Tump and sang a few hymns.

Fred Boughton remembers a good time with his family when he was a child. He was born in the Forest of Dean, Gloucestershire, in 1897. His father was a miner.

13 Special occasions

All families, whether they were rich or poor, celebrated special occasions. These might be private, family affairs like a wedding. They might be village or street occasions like a party or an outing. Whatever the occasion, men, women and children put on their best clothes and, usually, had fun. They remembered these occasions for years afterwards as something special they had enjoyed with their friends and family.

Source A

All the children in the parish between the ages of seven and eleven were by this time assembled. The girls who possessed them wearing white or light coloured frocks, and girls and boys decked out with bright ribbon knots. The queen wore her daisy crown with a white veil thrown over it. The procession stepped out briskly. The first stop was the **Rectory**. The garland was planted before the front door and the shrill little voices began to sing. The **Rector**'s face, would appear at an upper window, and nod in admiration and approval of the garland. His daughter slipped a silver coin into the collecting box, and the procession moved on towards the **Squire**'s. There, the lady of the house would bow haughty approval. The Squire himself would appear in the stable doorway. 'How many are there of you?' he would call. 'Twenty-seven? Well, here's a **five-bob bit** for you. Don't quarrel over it. Now let's have a song.'

Flora Thompson was born in 1876 at Juniper Hill, a village in Oxfordshire. In 1939 she wrote a book, *Lark Rise*, about her childhood. This is part of what she remembered about May Day celebrations in the village.

Source B

The first thing I remember was standing on a table in the nursery in a red frock and being told that it was my birthday and that I was three years old. I can see that red frock still. Perhaps one remembers earliest the things that one cares for most. Certainly I have always had a love for colour.

This is Mary Marshall's first memory of a special occasion. She was born in 1850, near Stamford in Lincolnshire. Her father was a country rector.

This picture was painted in 1889 by Stanhope Alexander Forbes. He called it *The Health of the Bride.*

My grandfather died in 1894 when I was ten years old. To me he was an old man and I couldn't feel sad. I was supposed to cry, and I did, with my elder sister Alice and my younger sister Rose. But I didn't really feel that something awful had happened. Grandfather had lived with us for as long as I could remember. His body was put in a coffin made from best oak. The coffin was put in our front room. All our friends and relatives came to see the body. There was a handkerchief over Grandfather's face. Mother sat by the coffin and took the handkerchief off for everyone who wanted to see his face. When it was all over, the lid was screwed down on the coffin. We children had to put on our best clothes and polish our shoes. We must have looked very smart at his funeral in the big, gloomy church at the end of our road in Islington. But I was very frightened because I couldn't remember his face.

Agnes Crane remembers her grandfather's funeral when she was ten years old.

GLOSSARY

black-lead a special polish for making the bars around grates shiny

cesspit a pit for liquid waste or sewage

chloroform a gas used by doctors to make people unconscious

cholera an infectious disease: a person with cholera usually died very quickly and in a lot of pain

clockwork coiled springs which, when wound up, uncoil to move the hands of a clock or the arms and legs of a toy

club a place where gentlemen could go to read the papers, talk to other gentlemen and have a meal

confidante a person to whom you could safely tell your secrets

diarrhoea human waste that is far more liquid than normal

disease illness

do-re-me board a system of music used to teach singing, painted on a special board

drayman a man who drove a brewer's cart laden with barrels and pulled by one or two horses

embroider to sew pictures or patterns in coloured threads

epidemic a disease which spreads quickly so that a lot of people have it at the same time

estate land belonging to a rich person

fire screen a screen put in front of a fire to stop the fire making people's faces too hot when they are sitting by it

five-bob bit a coin that was worth five shillings (twenty-five pence)

foundry-man a man who worked in an iron foundry

germ a tiny organism which carries disease

governess a woman teacher who taught rich children in their own homes

grate a frame of metal bars holding a fire in a fireplace

House of Lords part of Parliament which is made up of all the dukes, earls, bishops and barons and which has to agree to Bills sent to them by the House of Commons before they can become law

inherit to own land or property when the person who originally owned it dies

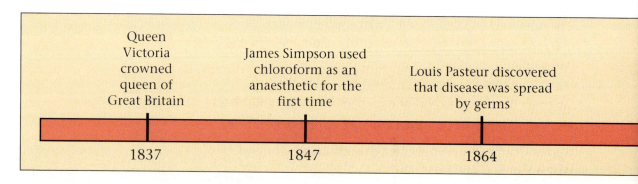

Queen Victoria crowned queen of Great Britain

James Simpson used chloroform as an anaesthetic for the first time

Louis Pasteur discovered that disease was spread by germs

1837   1847   1864

insanitary dirty

lice a tiny insect that lives in people's hair

landlord a person who owns land or property and who lets it out for rent

liqueurs sweet alcholic drinks

mill type of factory where things such as cotton were made

polluted made dirty

privy a lavatory which, in early Victorian times, would not have been connected to a sewer or flushed with water

rector a parish priest

rectory a house where a rector and his family live

refuse waste or rubbish

rent money paid to a landlord for land or a house or cottage

scarlet fever an infectious disease with a fever and red spots

servants' hall a large room where servants ate their meals and relaxed

sewer a pipe taking waste away from a lavatory or a sink

squire a country gentleman

squalid dirty, filthy, wretched to look at

stand-pipe an upright pipe, with a tap, joined in to a water main

stonemason a person who builds with stone

tenant a person who rents land or property

terraced house a house joined on both sides by other houses

town council people who are elected to run a town

tram a sort of bus that ran on rails in the road

tutor a man who taught boys, and sometimes their sisters as well, in their own homes

typhus fever a fever which can be passed on by touch

workhouse a place where the very poor went for food and shelter

Public Health Act: Councils were allowed to order slums to be pulled down. A Public Health Committee in each district provided water and got rid of sewage and rubbish.

John James Sainsbury opened his first multiple-grocery shop in Croydon, Surrey. Sainsburys shops spread through London and the south of England.

Death of Queen Victoria

1875   1882   1901

INDEX

Plain numbers (3) refer to the text and written sources. Italic numbers (*3*) refer to a picture.